The Happy Bookers

Books by Richard Armour

The Happy Bookers
It All Started with Columbus
It All Started with Europa
It All Started with Eve
It All Started with Freshman English
It All Started with Hippocrates
It All Started with Marx
It All Started with Stones and Clubs
My Life with Women
Out of My Mind
A Safari into Satire
A Short History of Sex
Through Darkest Adolescence
Twisted Tales from Shakespeare
Writing Light Verse
Writing Light Verse and Prose Humor

For All Ages
All in Sport
Our Presidents
The Strange Dreams of Rover Jones

For Children
The Adventures of Egbert the Easter Egg
All Sizes and Shapes of Monkeys and Apes
Animals on the Ceiling
A Dozen Dinosaurs
Odd Old Mammals
On Your Marks: A Package of Punctuation
Sea Full of Whales
Who's in Holes?
The Year Santa Went Modern

A Playful History of Librarians
and Their World from the
Stone Age to the
Distant Future

The
Happy
Bookers

by Richard Armour

With Appropriate Illustrations
by Campbell Grant

McGraw-Hill Book Company

New York Toronto St Louis Düsseldorf Mexico Panama

Book design by Paulette Nenner.

23456789BPBP79876

Library of Congress Cataloging in Publication Data

Armour, Richard Willard, 1906–
    The happy bookers.

    1.   Libraries—History—Anecdotes, facetiae, satire, etc. 2.   Librarians—Anecdotes, facetiae, satire, etc. 3.   Printing—History—Anecdotes, facetiae, satire, etc.
I.   Grant, Campbell, date   II.   Title.
Z721.A795   020.92′2   75-28313
ISBN 0-07-002303-4

Dedicated
to librarian-scholar-author John David Marshall,
who insisted that I write this book,
to my librarian son, Geoff (named after Geoffrey Chaucer),
and to all librarians,
since they are my favorite people.

Contents

The Happy Bookers

I

The Stone Age

*R*eading was at a low ebb in the Stone Age. Days were too filled with activity, such as pursuing some small animal that, if caught, would be the *pièce de résistance* of dinner. Or, quite as often, fleeing some large animal, such as a saber-toothed tiger, to escape being *its* dinner. There was no time to read until night, and then the light was too poor in the average cave.[1]

Moreover, with no newspapers or magazines there were no reviews. Nor was there a best-seller list. With no television there were no guest appearances by authors, plugging their books. How was anyone to know what was worth reading?

There were critics, but they were critics not of literary works but of the bad manners of people in other tribes, howling animals that kept them awake at night, lack of medical and dental care, poor community planning, with caves altogether too close to one another, and inflated prices, paid in hard-earned shells. Pessimism, even cynicism, was rampant, and there was much nostalgia for the Good Old Days.

Nonetheless the Stone Age librarian did the best

[1] Or even in the above-average cave.

he or she could to be of service. It was fairly easy to become a librarian, since it was not necessary to get an M.L.S. Inasmuch as there was no such thing as a Graduate School of Library Science, it was not only not necessary but not possible to get such a degree. The librarian thus escaped courses in Cataloging, Reference Materials, Library Administration, and the like. It would have been even more gratifying to the librarian to know what was missed by missing such courses.

The earliest library was in a cave within walking distance of the librarian's own cave. Since the horse had not yet been domesticated and this was before the invention of the wheel, the librarian's proximity to the library

was of more importance than it was later to become. Only a short walk over stones and fallen tree trunks, and the librarian was at the place of work.

As for the hour of arrival, this was somewhat difficult to ascertain, since there was as yet no such thing as a watch or clock, or even an hourglass or a sundial. But everyone went to bed early and got up early, and it was agreed that the librarian should be at work at sunrise. The only strict requirement, then as now, was that the ordinary librarian be on the job before the Head Librarian.[1] He could come in at almost any hour, going straight

[1]Not a keeper of heads, except in some cannibal tribes.

Pursuit

to his office after a quick look to make sure that all the librarians were at their posts.[1]

In the modern library the maintaining of display cases, including thinking up new displays, is usually a minor duty of some minor member of the library staff. Such a librarian, who thinks she is doing enough already, finds this extra assignment a troublesome chore. Instead of being changed once a month, displays may remain unchanged for six months or even a year. If this happens, the librarian may be reprimanded by the Head Librarian.

"You should display more," the Head Librarian may say, and the librarian is sometimes not certain whether the Head Librarian refers to the display cases or her manner of dress.[2]

However, things were quite different in the Stone Age library. There were no display cases, but the visual element was provided by paintings on the sides of the cave walls. They were a major rather than a minor part of the library, many persons coming in to see these works of art rather than to take out a book. Once the walls were covered by carvings and paintings there was no need, or even any possibility, of changing the exhibits.

[1]There really were posts in many libraries, propping up caves that had become insecure from erosion and landslides during an exceptionally rainy season.

[2]"I draw the line," the librarian may say, having her neckline or hemline in mind.

Major part of the library

The Happy Bookers

The librarian assigned to this extra duty had very little to do except to guard the art works from being tampered with by envious artists or the adding of initials or embarrassing graffiti.[1] The pictorial material was of special benefit to the Children's Librarian, who could hold the attention of Beginning Readers by pointing out and telling stories, during Story Hour, about some of the Stone Age animals depicted, such as the woolly rhinoceros, the mammoth, and the cave bear. This librarian

[1]Some might be obscene, causing trouble with the Library Board, but even such harmless scribblings as "Glog was here" were frowned upon.

Casually draped over the shoulder

The Happy Bookers

would skillfully divert the attention of impressionable youngsters from the bloodier hunting scenes and from men and women who were not sufficiently covered by the crude clothing of the day, when animal fur was used for more than women's coats and stoles. Furs were draped casually over the shoulder and were intended more for warmth than for fashion or cover.

But back to the Delivery Desk. Since there were

Clumsy reader

no books, people had to content themselves with rectangular stones that were recommended by the librarian or by friends who had taken them out.[1] Anyone holding a library card, made of tree bark, could take out as many as four stones and keep them for two weeks.[2] There was no card attached to the stone, nor was there a rubber stamp to stamp the card with the date due. But the librarian could scratch an identifying mark with a piece of flint, and

[1]Kidney stones and gallstones had not yet been taken out, though this was the Stone Age.

[2]How they could tell when the two weeks were up, without a calendar, is hard to figure out. Perhaps in the Old Stone Age, or Paleolithic Period, book borrowers simply kept track of the number of times the sun came up and went down. Some mistakes may have been made on cloudy days, and fines had to be paid for overdue stones.

this was done with the professional skill for which librarians were known even in those Early Days.[1]

Once they had returned to their own cave, patrons of the library made good use of the stones they had borrowed. Since there was no cave door to prop open or pile of papers to be held down on a desk, they could not use the stones as many use books in Modern Times. But they could gain status among their friends by asking them whether they had seen the latest stone, knowing full well they could not have, since they had been the first to take out the library's only copy. And they could take a library stone to bed with them and gaze blankly at its blankness until they were sufficiently bored to go to sleep.

Stone Age people did not have the expression "to throw the book" at someone, but they were familiar with "a stone's throw" as a measure of distance as well as the more moralistic injunction about "casting the first stone." Any such activity was of course frowned upon by the librarian, who carefully examined each stone when it was returned and looked for signs of mistreatment.

Cataloging of these rectangular stones was difficult, since this was before either the Dewey Decimal System or the Library of Congress method, but librarians even in those days were resourceful, and they found a

---

[1] A deep mark indicated friction and a shallow mark nonfriction.

way. They also knew when someone had foolishly tried to replace a stone in the stacks instead of leaving it out for the librarian to place precisely where it belonged.

Happily, there was no rustling of paper, and there was always quiet in the Reading Room—unless a clumsy reader dropped a stone on the floor. This would incense the librarian, who would reprimand the reader and ask that there be consideration for others.

The librarian loved his work, safe in the cave-library from wild animals and even wilder tribesmen. It was required that clubs be left outside, in the club rack, and there were to be no infractions of the rules established by the Library Board. Support, in the form of posts and beams, was given by the Friends of the Library, a loyal group consisting of some of the leaders of the community. Dues were a modest number of shells, though those wishing to give more were listed as Patrons. They met as often as once a year and through their efforts made it possible to add a wing to the cave. The library was one of the few caves with a wing. The hope was that it would eventually have two wings and be able to fly, taking books to out-of-the-way places much as does the modern Bookmobile.

Libraries underwent many such changes during the Upper Paleolithic and Neolithic periods. Librarians, however, remained as modest and hard-working and efficient and low-salaried as ever.

II

Librarians in Mesopotamia

By around 4000 B.C. libraries had moved out of caves and into temples and royal palaces, and librarians gained such respect as they have not had since. The reason for this was that they were among the few who could read, and library patrons instead of asking "Where is it?" would ask "What does it say?"

This happened in Mesopotamia, which was occupied successively by the Sumerians, the Babylonians, and the Assyrians. Byron was probably unfamiliar with the history of the book when he wrote his famous line, "The Assyrian came down like the wolf on the fold," since in those early days not even a librarian could fold the pages of a book, books being clay tablets.[1]

Not only were they clay tablets, considerably larger than cough tablets, but they were covered with pictographs, which were little pictures that served the purpose of words. For instance a drawing of a wolf meant "wolf," and a wolf with its mouth wide open and teeth showing could mean either "hungry wolf" or "dangerous wolf," the two being synonymous.

---

[1]Lighter and easier to handle, however, than the rectangular stones of the Stone Age.

These clay tablets were baked, like bread, but fortunately for librarians were not edible. Also by the time they were delivered to the library they had cooled and were not too hot to handle.[1]

Somewhat later, pictographs were supplanted by cuneiform writing, which was considered more stylish because it was written with a stylus. The letters or characters, inscribed in clay, were mostly wedge shaped and looked something like the handwriting on a doctor's prescription. But librarians, who in those days could claim a kinship with pharmacists, were capable of deciphering such writing.

Librarianship took an upward leap when librarians learned to place needed works where they could be found only by a qualified librarian. A favorite place for depositing (hiding) a popular work was in an earthen jar. Anyone wishing to find such a tablet had to seek out the librarian and humbly ask, "Which jar is it in?" This gave the librarian something to do and justified a place in the sun.[2]

Next to come was the cataloging of books, or clay tablets. These were classified in such main categories as Gods, Legends, Omens, Charms, Kings, Wars, and

[1]Some of them contained heated remarks, which remained rather warm.

[2]Or, on a hot day in what was later to become Iraq, in the shade.

The Happy Bookers

Librarians in Mesopotamia

How to bake a book

The Happy Bookers

Incantations. Under the heading of History were accounts of the Old Days, the most popular being about the Flood. It made the present seem better.

As for gods, the patron god of librarians was Nabu, or Nebo, who also looked out for scribes and schools. If a librarian made a horrible mistake, such as incorrectly cataloging a tablet, and cried out, "Oh, my

Which jar?

god!" it was probably Nabu who was being called upon and not the Head Librarian.

Specialization entered the life of librarians with Hammurabi, about 1950 B.C. He was not only King of Babylonia but responsible for the Code of Hammurabi, or at least for its name. This was a codification of laws, and what is of interest to librarians is that it made possible the first law library.[1] Once this was established, medical libraries, science libraries, and all the rest were assured, thus creating more jobs for librarians. Law librarians should never forget what they owe to Hammurabi, and include him with Nabu in their prayers.

Libraries at first were private, open only to royalty and priests. But around 1000 B.C. the Assyrians opened their libraries to the public. Anyone could use them, including some whom librarians could do without. In connection with public libraries, a name to remember is King Ashurbanipal, who developed a library of over 30,000 tablets. Though it was in his palace and not called the Nineveh Public Library, that was what it really was. The Friends of the Nineveh Public Library were friends, or retainers, of Ashurbanipal, and must have been proud of the ingenious way the palace library was organized into rooms for tablets on different subjects.

When Nineveh was destroyed by the invading

[1]Or legal library, though this is not to suggest that other libraries are illegal.

The Happy Bookers

Chaldeans and Scythians in 612 B.C., the library was burned down, but no harm was done to the already well-done clay tablets. Not the same, however, can be said of any librarians who may have stubbornly remained at

Read them right there

their desks because it was not yet closing time.

✳ In Babylonia a librarian was known not as a librarian but as a "Tablet Keeper." This was all right for a librarian but not for a user of the library, probably known as a "Tablet Borrower." In fact a user of the library very likely could not take tablets out at all, but had to read them right there. As has been mentioned earlier, in the Stone Age a stone could be checked out by the librarian with a piece of flint, but a clay tablet might chip off or even crack right down the middle if a librarian tried to hammer into it the date due.

In the libraries of Mesopotamia, both Babylonian and Assyrian, circulation of tablets was necessarily limited. "Come in and read during Open Hours," the librarian would say, "but leave your tablet close to its jar."[1]

Some think speed reading is a recent development, but I am not so sure. I have just read of a people who lived in the area that is now part of Syria called the Hurrians. Perhaps they were so named because of the speed with which they read, or then again they may have vexed the librarians of that era with demands for quick service.

Even working in a palace and with a benevolent Trustee such as Ashurbanipal, librarianship has never been easy.

[1]As a hint, the lid of the jar was kept ajar.

III

Librarians in Ancient Egypt

*L*ibrarians who lived in Egypt from about 3000 B.C. to 1500 B.C.[1] experienced considerable change in the books or tablets they handled. For one thing, pictographic writing was carved on stones rather than on clay, and some thought they might be going back to the Stone Age instead of making progress. However, they did change the name from pictographic to hieroglyphic writing, which gave them the kind of satisfaction librarians get from doing something innovative. But lifting stone tablets also gave rise, or fall, to hernias, and librarians began to take more sick leave.

All writing was not done on stone, however. Leather and papyrus came into use. Thanks to leather, some books, as Francis Bacon later wrote, could be "chewed and digested" (which could also be done with bacon), and librarians had to keep a sharp eye out for hungry patrons. As for papyrus, it made a rustling sound when pages were turned, despite all the signs saying "Silence" and "Quiet," and librarians bit their fingernails with frustration.[2]

[1]Those were some of the longer-lived librarians.

[2]They also used their teeth.

With these new materials came other forms of writing. Passing over the hieratic and demotic, we believe a truly modern touch was given to books with what was called cursive writing. In addition to flowing along nicely, cursive writing was, as its name suggests, ideal for writing obscenities, which were as popular in Ancient Egypt as today. Librarians had to check everything cursive very closely, first savoring it themselves and then surreptitiously slipping it to members of the royal family, priests, and others whose minds could not be polluted.[1]

[1]Or whose minds were already so polluted that nothing could make them any more so.

Heavy reading

The Happy Bookers

The temple and palace libraries of Egypt were under the direction not of a Head Librarian but someone known as a "Controller of the Library" or "Keeper of the Scrolls." These of course were men, usually scribes. That meant they were highly trained, being able not only to read but to write. A scroll, which is etymologically if in no other way related to a scrotum, was a piece of papyrus with cursive writing on it that was rolled up into a cylinder when not being read. This was something that was hard to do with a stone or clay tablet.

A librarian carrying a tightly rolled scroll had a

Unrolling a scroll

forbidding appearance, looking a little like a policeman with a club. Patrons were quiet and well behaved, at least while the librarian was watching them.[1]

The temple library was both a library school, or place for on-the-job training, and a library. Some of these libraries had names that only a librarian could pronounce, such as Edfu, Thoth (named by a priest with a lisp), and Ptah. It was at Thoth, it should be noted, that perhaps the first woman rose above the lowest rank of librarians, becoming known as "Mistress of the House of Books." She was still not in charge, being an assistant to the priest, who was "Keeper of the Sacred Books." Nor is this to suggest that, though her title was Mistress, she was a mistress of the priest. At any rate it was thousands of years until a woman was to rise again to such eminence in the field of librarianship.[2]

In a sense, the pyramids of ancient Egypt were libraries. That is, papyrus sheets and rolls have been found in virtually all the tombs. Some of these were guidebooks that told the deceased where he could go.[3]

[1]Scrolls were kept in pigeonholes, which the pigeons had been forced to vacate.

[2]That some librarians may have been the mistresses of secular, or sexular, Head Librarians is possible, but digression on this subject would lead us away from the professional character of this book.

[3]He may have been told this while alive but was too annoyed to pay much attention.

The Happy Bookers

Often his favorite works were buried with him, now that he had plenty of time for reading and not much else to do. It was quiet down there also, but the light was none too good.

The only librarians in the pyramids, however, were dead librarians, used to fill in cracks and corners not occupied by the late King. This was all right with the librarian, who could not have got in otherwise and wanted to be useful right to the end.

The greatest library of Egypt and of Early Times was the Alexandrian Library. It is best known for having

Parting gift

The Happy Bookers

been destroyed. This is so much emphasized that it is sometimes forgotten, except by librarians, that before it was destroyed it was built.[1]

[1] In *The Alexandrian Library,* Edward Alexander (note that middle name) Parsons devotes 156 pages to the destruction of the library. Seldom has so much been written about so little remaining.

Book burning becomes a fad

Alexander the Great founded the city of Alexandria, but Ptolemy I, the King of Egypt, founded the library in the third century B.C.[1] It became the largest and most famous collection of books in the ancient world, growing to about 700,000 volumes, thanks to accessions by both

[1]The "P" in Ptolemy is silent, which should please librarians.

The Happy Bookers

gifts and conquest, and employing no telling how many catalogers.

But back to that matter of greatest importance, how the Alexandrian Library was destroyed. Librarians will, I know, find it exciting reading and (1) be glad they were not there and (2) hope the same thing does not happen to their own library.

Julius Caesar was probably the first to start the destruction of the library, but there is a difference of opinion among such historians as Seneca, Plutarch, Suetonius, Livy, Orosius, Gibbon, and Will Durant, to mention only a few, regarding the nature and extent of Caesar's depredations. Some think all Caesar did was take home with him some books given him by Cleopatra, who hoped thereby, if she had not been able to do so otherwise, to indicate her love for him.[1]

Others believe that only part of the library was burned, by accident, when Caesar set fire to some ships in the harbor. Still others maintain that Caesar completely destroyed the library, indeed "sacking" it, presumably carrying off the 700,000 volumes in book bags brought for the purpose.

One way or another, Caesar seems to have

[1]According to those who hold to this theory, the librarians were climbing the walls (which may have been the real cause of destruction of the library) with each rare book Cleopatra took from the Treasure Room and insisted Caesar take along.

started what almost became a fad. The Alexandrian Library was to some extent burned, ransacked, or defiled[1] by Caracalla, Gallienus, Zenobia, Diocletian, Theophilus, Omar, and 'Amr.[2] But though this may have been the beginning of what we know today as book burning, the Alexandrian Library kept rising from the ashes. It might have been easier to have protected the books had they remained as stones and clay tablets. But there always seemed to be a new supply of papyrus. Had there not been this repeated destruction of the Alexandrian Library and other libraries, there might now be such a surplus of books as would make it difficult for authors and publishers to survive.

Speaking of survival, I must express my dismay that in all their concern about the loss of books in the Alexandrian Library, none of the historians has anything to say about the librarians quietly cataloging and doing reference work while the flames drew closer and closer.

Librarians care about historians. Don't historians care about librarians?

[1]I.e., the files removed.

[2]Omar's lieutenant, whose name is disconcertingly like Armour.

IV

Librarians in Greece and Rome

Librarians in ancient Greece were highly educated. They could read and speak Greek fluently.

Though there were clay and papyrus books in Greece as early as 1400 B.C., writing seems to have disappeared temporarily because of incursions by barbarians from the north.[1] For several centuries the people of Greece had no written language. This included the era of Homer, and we are told by one scholar that "the *Iliad* and the *Odyssey* were composed and handed down as oral epics for many generations before they were finally written down."

How something oral is handed from one person to another is not explained. What concerns us, however, is the function of the librarian at a time when there was nothing in writing. Perhaps the librarian listened to someone recite, over and over, the lines of Homer's great epics. Then, after learning them by heart,[2] the librarian

[1] Barbaric conquerors, you will notice, almost always "sweep down from the north." They rarely sweep up from the south. At least the Greeks should have known the direction from which the invaders were coming.

[2] Or by head.

instead of lending a patron the desired works would say, "Lend me your ear." Thereupon the librarian would recite as much of the *Iliad* or the *Odyssey* as the patron could stand.

Fortunately for authors, readers, and librarians, written works were available again by the seventh century B.C. Thereupon, we are told, "libraries sprung up all

Greek epic

The Happy Bookers

over Greece." It would have been interesting, and a little frightening, to see them coming up like mushrooms. One might be standing on a spot where a library chose to spring up, and the next minute be on the roof, or at least on a pillar or a pediment.[1]

While there were temple and palace libraries, there were also collections in upper-class homes. One exhaustive piece of research turned up a papyrus work in excellent condition. There was great excitement among the excavators. Translators found it to be the grocery list for a large household. Anyone interested can probably find it in one of the libraries of Egypt today, proudly pointed out by the guides as one of the treasures of antiquity. However, it might be something of a problem for a librarian to catalog.

One of the earliest builders of a public library in Athens is said to have been Pisistratus (605–527 B.C.).[2] Pisistratus is known as "the tyrant of Athens," and yet he was a builder of temples, a lover of the arts, and a supporter of the poor. Of most interest to librarians, however, was his starting the city library of Athens by presenting his personal collection. Perhaps what is

[1]An admirer of Greek culture would not wish to be an impediment to a pediment.

[2]Another source gives his dates as 612–527 B.C. Birth and death dates are important to a librarian but even more important to the person involved.

needed in the development of libraries is more tyrants, especially those with large collections of books which they are willing to give away as a tax deduction. No one is suggesting any need for more tyrants among Library Trustees, Head Librarians, or professors in library schools.

Many of the Greek libraries were not actually in Greece but in Egypt (i.e., the Alexandrian Library), Pergamum, and other areas taken over during the conquests of Alexander the Great, who is supposed to have carried a copy of the *Iliad* with him wherever he went. It is said that Achilles was Alexander's hero and model, but it may actually have been that Alexander used the book to protect him from spears or from the slings and arrows of outrageous fortune. A metal shield might have been more effective, but a work as long as the *Iliad,* written on vellum, would have provided adequate protection without causing Alexander to appear cowardly.

Though it may have been used earlier, parchment came to replace papyrus at Pergamum during a papyrus shortage.[1] Parchment, as any librarian knows who has taken a course in History of the Book, is material pre-

[1]The supply of papyrus was cut off when the rulers of Egypt became jealous of the way the library of Pergamum was growing and fearful that it might become larger than the Alexandrian. This sort of rivalry among libraries continues to exist, but it is usually settled by a battle of book budgets rather than troops.

The Happy Bookers

pared from the skin of various animals, especially the sheep, the calf, and the goat. It was not widely used until about 200 B.C. Then it became the favorite writing material in Europe for many centuries, in fact until the invention of paper. Librarians liked parchment, because it was tougher than papyrus and would stand even the abuse given it by the average patron. Indeed parchment until recently was used in diplomas, which were appropriately called "sheepskins."[1] Now that colleges have fallen on hard times, however, the graduate is fortunate to have his degree on a good-grade rag bond.

[1]The B.A. was often pronounced, sheepishly, "Baa."

Looking for parchment

The Happy Bookers

But back to Athens. It is said that by the third century B.C. one scholar, Timaeus, the Sicilian historian,[1] spent fifty years doing research in libraries. Of course he may have got lost or have stayed after closing hours and been locked in.

Besides all the other types, there were also medical libraries, in connection with medical schools. It is said that one such library was burned down by Hippocrates, who was annoyed because his students refused to obey his teachings.[2] Today it is usually the students rather than the teacher who burn down a school or a library. However the effect is the same, and it proves how much you can lose if you lose your temper.

Rome

One of the problems for librarians in Rome was the toga. This costume made it possible for unscrupulous library patrons to hide the scrolls of papyrus and sheets of

[1]With whom you are no doubt familiar. I must confess I had never heard of him until I read Elmer D. Johnson's *A History of Libraries in the Western World,* which tells everything I had always wondered about libraries but was afraid to ask a librarian, even in a whisper.

[2]See the present author's *It All Started with Hippocrates,* a history of medicine which fails to mention this.

parchment underneath and carry them away without being checked out. Unfortunately neither the turnstyle nor the x-ray scanner had as yet been invented, and losses must have been considerable.

But advances were made too. Most noteworthy was the alphabet, which began in the Western World with the Phoenicians, Greeks, and Etruscans and made great strides with the Romans.[1] The first Roman letters were all capitals, perhaps because Rome itself was capital of the Roman Empire, but out of regard for the lower classes the alphabet soon was written in lower case also. All of this of course meant a great deal to the ultimate development of printing as well as to books as we now know them, and above all to librarians. On card files especially, it is a help to find under Subject or Author Ca-Cl or Pi-Pr instead of crude pictographs.[2]

Acquisitions to the early Roman libraries were largely made as the Roman legions conquered great areas of Asia Minor, Greece, Italy, and other parts of the world. It can be safely said, or at least one distinguished historian says it, that "Rome's first major libraries proba-

[1] You may have heard someone called a walking encyclopedia, but you may never have seen the letters of the alphabet striding along vigorously.

[2] It also helps the librarian, as well as the reader, to have to learn only twenty-six letters instead of the 15,000 or so characters needed by the Chinese scholar.

The Happy Bookers

bly were acquired as spoils of war." It is a pity that Roman soldiers were not as well trained in librarianship as in the arts of war, since they destroyed many valuable manuscripts and sometimes brought back slaves instead of longer-lasting books.

Nonetheless enough writings were included in the

Unscrupulous patrons

The Happy Bookers

loot to establish some notable private libraries in Rome. Indeed one general, Paulus Aemilius, preferred books to gold, and brought back enough books to establish a substantial collection. Other generals followed his example, and soon books were flowing into Rome from all over the Empire. This way of building up libraries made Friends of the Library and donors unnecessary, and there

Free back scrub

are those who now long for the Good Old Days, when there was no need for benefits, book auctions, or keeping within the budget.

Julius Caesar had the idea of establishing a public library in Rome, but was assassinated before it was completed. Contrary to rumor, he was not assassinated by the Enemies of the Public Library. These were disgruntled

The Happy Bookers

Romans who found the book they wanted usually charged out to someone else, had to pay a fine for returning a book a couple of days late, or disliked a book that had been enthusiastically recommended by the librarian.

The first public library was established by C. Asinius Pollio,[1] who had become wealthy by ravaging nearby countries—in those days the surest way to riches and fame. Starting with Augustus, best known for giving us the name of the month of August, public libraries in Rome were largely built by Emperors. This is true of Tiberius, Trajan, Hadrian, and others. Trajan's library was later transferred to the Baths of Diocletian, and librarians who delivered books to patrons often threw in a free back scrub.

In the latter part of the Roman era Christian libraries began to emerge. They gave something to Christians to do while waiting to be thrown to the lions, and Christian librarians were kept busy when not praying that they themselves be spared. From time to time these libraries were destroyed by anti-Christian Romans, but the blazes were spectacular and brought many curious onlookers.[2]

[1]Pollio flourished in the first century B.C., long before the discovery of Salk vaccine.

[2]The most curious were those who stayed around and were converted. There may have been a shortage of sackcloth, but not of ashes.

Tyrannion, who despite his name was quite a decent fellow, was one of the early librarians of Rome. Like many other librarians, he was a well-educated scholar who was taken prisoner during a Roman foray and brought back as a slave. Since he was better at reading and cataloging papyrus than at doing something useful, such as sweeping streets, they put him in charge of a library. Later, on obtaining his freedom, he left the library and became a trader in books and an adviser to such dictators and public speakers as Sulla and Cicero. Anyone who thinks librarianship is the end of the road should remember Tyrannion.

The libraries of Rome were cataloged by subject and author, Greek and Latin works were separated, and there was other evidence that the modern library was well on its way. For instance there was that *sine qua non* of today's library, censorship. The Emperor Augustus ordered the works of Ovid removed from library shelves, presumably because they lacked redeeming social value. And Pope Gregory I is said to have suppressed the works of Cicero and Livy because young men (and perhaps also young women) were wasting their time reading such things when they should have been reading the Bible. Before Christians came into power the works of Christians were banned, and when Christians became dominant the works of non-Christians were suppressed.[1]

[1]There is a certain even-handedness and equality of intolerance in this.

The Happy Bookers

Too busy for reading

During the Decline of the Roman Empire people were too busy with orgies to do much reading, and libraries also declined. After the Fall and with the coming of the Dark Ages, the light was too poor and libraries and librarians were at their lowest point.[1]

[1]This, of course, will be disputed by a few disgruntled librarians today.

V

Librarians in the Middle Ages

More is known about middle-aged librarians than about librarians in the Middle Ages. Of course there were middle-aged librarians in the Middle Ages, but they thought of themselves as medieval librarians, a confusing description which they perhaps used on purpose.

Skipping over the Byzantine and Moslem libraries, including those of Constantinople, Baghdad, Damascus, and Samarkand, and thereby saving a good many pages, we come to the monastic libraries of the Middle Ages in Europe.[1] These were no great shakes, compared to the libraries of Rome before the Fall, but they gave monks something to do besides pray for forgiveness after having evil thoughts about some of the young nuns in the nearby nunnery.

The library in a medieval monastery at first had only a few codices.[2] These were ancient manuscripts,

---

[1] We cannot pass over the fact that wealthy Arabs are said to have owned so many camel-loads of books. The first requisite of a well-trained librarian was the ability to ride a camel and decipher the catalog numbers during the severest sandstorm.

[2] If it had only one, it was a codex, that being the singular, and it really didn't make a very impressive library.

usually written in the Greek minuscule hand and very hard on the eyes. Though made of papyrus, they were in book form rather than rolls and gave the librarian the idea of placing them side by side instead of into holes. The modern library was beginning to take shape, and it was only a question of time until there would be bookplates, bookmarks, book ends, bookcases, and bookworms, both the insect and the human variety. Mostly these

Scribe in scriptorium

The Happy Bookers

books were Scriptural texts, appropriate to a monastery, and the sexy passages were deleted after having been read several times by the head monk. The oldest codices were called *codices vetustissimi,* and were obviously superlative. The librarian hovered around, prepared to pick up the pieces if the manuscript fell apart.

Until the invention of printing, books or manuscripts were written by hand.[1] Monasteries therefore served not only as libraries but as printers, binders, and publishing houses, since it was in the monasteries that monks who served as scribes produced these handwritten books.[2] Scribes were not members of a union, but then again in a sense they were, since they were subject to the rules of the monastery. They worked in a room known as a *scriptorium,* and were protected from interruption except by high officials.[3] If they were even momentarily distracted from their meticulous work they might misspell a word, leave one out, or put in a negative that would completely change the meaning.

The work of a scribe on a manuscript was final. There were no galley proofs or page proofs, and in the case of a classic the author might have been dead a

[1]Anyone who does not know that "manuscript" comes from the Latin *manu scriptus,* "written by hand," isn't a librarian.

[2]Copying, in those days, was not considered plagiarism.

[3]Persons of authority, not those who had imbibed too much.

thousand years and hardly in a position[1] to do any proofreading.

The *scriptorium* was officiated over by a librarian known as the *armarius,* who may or may not have been armed but whose duty it was to provide parchment, pens, ink, knives, rulers, and awls.[2] That the scribes were also at least librarians in training we know from the fact that the most important rule in the *scriptorium* was absolute silence. According to Douglas C. McMurtrie, in *The Book,* "If a scribe wished to consult a book, he made certain signs to his fellow workers. For example, in asking for a pagan work, he made the general sign, followed by scratching the ear in the manner of a dog!"[3]

Although what we refer to as audio-visual had not yet entered the library scene, the visual was much in evidence in medieval manuscripts, many of which were illuminated by colorful drawings, either in the first letter of a new sentence or in the margins. Others were illuminated more spectacularly. In fact the whole sky was illuminated when libraries, monastic or otherwise, were set afire by illiterate barbarians who (see above) had

---

[1] Flat on his back.

[2] "Awl or nothing," the *armarius* might say, if in an ugly mood.

[3] McMurtrie does not tell us what sign the scribe-librarian made, or what part of his anatomy he scratched, if he wished to consult a Christian work.

The Happy Bookers

Sub cathedra

swept down from the north.

It was in the Irish monasteries that manuscripts became noted for some of the finest calligraphy and illumination. The *Book of Kells,* for example, has been hailed as the most beautiful book in the world, more beautiful for instance than the *Book of Martyrs* (at least more pleasant reading) or Thackeray's *Book of Snobs.* Any librarian whose library possesses the original manuscript of the *Book of Kells* very likely works at the library of Trinity College, Dublin. And if you ask to sign it out for two weeks you may notice as strange a facial expression as you have ever seen.

Larger than the monastery libraries, and providing more opportunities for librarians, were the cathedral libraries. It was a little like the difference between college and university libraries today. The cathedral libraries had more funds for the acquisition of books, these funds coming from flattering the wealthy or frightening the poor.[1] There were also more secular books in the cathedral library, since the monks in a monastery were supposed to be interested only in reading religious works. On the other hand, all sorts of people came to the cathedral and therefore were interested in all sorts of books, some

---

[1]Monastery libraries were sometimes so small that the ratio of one book per monk was considered rather good. So far as is known, there was no Book-of-the-Monk Club.

The Happy Bookers

of which were slipped to them not *ex cathedra* but *sub cathedra*.[1]

A monastic librarian was known not only as an *armarius* but as a *bibliothecarius* and a *custos librorum*. This last term did not mean that the librarian cussed

[1]The monks might have been interested too, but they sublimated their interest by praying, telling their beads (no telling what), and shaving the top of each other's head.

Deposit required

books but that he was the custodian of books. Sometimes the librarian was old or unwell and unable to perform any more demanding duty. He might also have some other obligation, such as watering the plants or dusting the altar, but by the time a monk became a *custos librorum* he knew he was over the hill and spent more and more time making suggestions about the inscription on his tomb.[1]

The interlibrary loan is nothing new. Books were lent to neighboring libraries to be copied and even to libraries in other countries. Also the lending of books to people in the community became more common. At first books could be lent only one at a time and had to be used somewhere near the monastery and only during daylight. If books were lent to strangers, a deposit was required. Those were not just the Middle Ages but the Good Old Days for nervous, untrusting librarians.

But permissiveness set in. Eventually books could be taken to the patron's living quarters and kept for as long as a year.[2] At least if the monastic library were destroyed, the books could be saved and perhaps a century later, when the Vandals or Huns or whoever had

[1] There was no such thing as retirement for the monastic librarian. When he finished his work he was finished.

[2] Can you imagine taking out a library book for a year? Of course, should the book be kept longer than a year there would be a small fine—so much for each year the book was overdue.

The Happy Bookers

left, they could be returned to the library, or the site of the library.[1]

By the twelfth century another kind of library began to appear in Europe. This was the university library. One of the earliest was the Sorbonne in Paris. This was followed by libraries at Oxford, Cambridge, and other centers of learning. The librarian was faced with a new and troublesome factor: the student. Wisely, at the

[1]Additional information about the monastery and cathedral libraries, if anything more needs to be known, can be found in such works as Léopold Delisle's *Recherches sur l'ancienne bibliothèque de Corbie* and Bernhard Bischoff's *Die süddeutschen Schreibschulen und Bibliotheken in der Karolingerzeit*, neither of which I have read.

Books were chained

Sorbonne books were chained to shelves, but the chains were long enough to reach to the desks where the books were read, and sometimes entangled the unwary student. At New College in Oxford an inventory was taken of all books each year.[1]

At the medieval universities there were no professional librarians. Usually the keeper of the books was a lesser faculty member or a student. Sometimes the librarian doubled as chaplain, or the chaplain doubled as a librarian, no doubt wearing a doublet and trying to remember when he was which. It would be embarrassing if a student came in for a book and got a blessing, or came in for a blessing and got a book. At least the blessing could be taken out without paying a deposit and could be kept indefinitely.

The librarian in a medieval university, such as Cracow or Heidelberg or Prague, might be a scholar who had actually read the books he dispensed or a person charged with keeping the books from being misplaced or mutilated, more aware of their physical condition than their contents.

The two kinds of librarians are with us today, almost six hundred years later. As someone probably said, about 1380, "It takes all kinds of librarians. . . ."[2]

[1]How many books were taken each year is not known.

[2]And people take out all kinds of books.

VI

Librarians and the Birth of Printing

It must not be assumed from the title of this chapter that librarians gave birth to printing. Nevertheless they were greatly affected when books were first printed instead of being copied by hand. At once it was possible to order, with a good chance that the order would be filled, any number of identical copies of a book.[1]

With printing, books (rolls of papyrus, codices of parchment) were no longer in manuscript form, precious rarities to be acquired chiefly by conquest and guarded in the libraries of fortified castles and sanctified monasteries. Nor were librarians forced to give a large part of their valuable time to acting as scribes or overseers of scribes. They could unashamedly display their fingernails, which had not a trace of the ink and coloring that once marked them as manual, manuscriptal, or manuscriptural laborers.

Once printed books became available, fewer and fewer librarians were monks, and almost none were nuns. A higher percentage of books, not produced in the local *scriptorium*, could be ordered direct from the

[1]Any number, that is, the budget would allow.

printer, and most of them would arrive in mint condition.[1] The number of books, or the volume of volumes, increased astronomically, and there were many more openings for catalogers. For a time, immediately after the coming of the printed book, there was no such thing as an unemployed librarian, even one who had not had at least three years' experience.[2]

Printing, as well as the making of paper, began in China as early as the fifth or sixth century. Subsequently it spread to Japan, along with typhus and other communicable diseases. The Chinese are also credited with inventing movable type long before Gutenberg, but they had so many characters to move around that they gave up on it. The Chinese printer who invented movable type was Pi Shêng. He preferred type made of baked clay to type made of wood, perhaps because he had an almost psychopathic fear of splinters.

It was in Korea, however, and not under Pi but under Yi, that fonts of metal type were created. Unlike Pi, Yi was not a printer but a General who took over the

[1]In the Old Days, sprigs of mint were used as bookmarks by those who preferred sniffing a book to reading it.

[2]Young librarians just out of Library School who must have experience to get a job and must first have a job to get experience, will find this incredible—especially when they have just run through the list of openings (usually closed by then) in the *Library Journal*.

The Happy Bookers

Pi

Government and during his enlightened administration encouraged the arts, including the printing of books. It should not be too much to ask of librarians that they remember the names of Pi and Yi, which lend themselves to memorization better than Gutenberg and Incunabula.

But enough of printing in Asia. This could be the subject of an entire book, one which I do not intend to write. Also I would have to do research on the Asian librarian, and the European librarian is trouble enough.[1]

One reason the early library had no periodicals room, in which the librarian was always trying to keep magazines and newspapers up to date, was that paper, which had been invented in China, was a thousand years getting to Europe.[2] Anything resembling a newspaper would have to be called a newspapyrus, a newsparchment, or a newsvellum. Also the slowness of making manuscripts, one copy at a time, would have made the news months or even years late. News traveled by word-of-mouth, which left libraries out of it, unless the librarian was known to be a well-informed gossip.

In the fourteenth century, printing in Europe began with the use of woodcuts. Many of the early woodcuts depicted religious scenes, but others, more useful but frowned upon in some quarters, were playing

[1]I shall also have something to say about the American librarian, never fear—unless you are an American librarian.

[2]No doubt on a very slow boat, perhaps a Chinese junk.

cards. Whether playing cards were used by librarians during rest periods, I have not been able to ascertain. The cards were printed with wooden blocks, and the printer was called a block printer, which at least was better than being called a blockhead.

The next step, in the early fifteenth century, was block printing by means of metal rather than wooden blocks. Whereas the wooden blocks were made by artistic carpenters, the metal blocks were made by goldsmiths who worked with the knife, the burin, and various punches and stamps. If you don't know what a burin is, it is high time you find out. Any librarian will direct you to some scholarly reference work on printing, though you can discover all you need to know in a good dictionary. There were, by the way, both punches and counterpunches, and watching a block printer at work must have been something like watching a boxing match.

Block books, with words as well as illustrations, were next. But except for those who liked to play with blocks, they were not wholly satisfactory. Printing with

Woodcutting

The Happy Bookers

blocks, even with good ink and on paper, was slow and dull. Until typography, which meant printing letter by letter with pieces of type, there was little or no opportunity for what was to be the most exciting feature of the printed book: the typographical error.

Think of the fun and games it brought to librarianship. Think of the laughter, the camaraderie, when the typographical error at last made its appearance! To spot a typographical error was, for a librarian, a joyous break in the daily routine.[1]

The inventor of movable type, which made all this possible, was probably Johann Gutenberg. I say probably because some scholars think it could or should have been someone else.[2] Moreover Gutenberg himself is a figure of controversy. Consider these facts. Out of five books on the history of printing:

(1) Two give his first name as Johann, two as Johannes, and one as "Johann or Henne."

(2) One says he was born "about 1397," one says

---

[1]Usually a spot is removed. "Out, damned spot!" Lady Macbeth cried with unladylike language. But in this instance something was spotted on purpose.

[2]See, for example, Jan Hendrick Hessels' *The Gutenberg Fiction; Showing That He Was Not the Inventor of Printing,* London, 1912. Or if you prefer to read something in Dutch, try Charles Enschedé's *Technisch onderzoek naar de uitvinding van de boekdrukkunst,* Haarlem, 1901. I am sure I would have found it fascinating if I could have found it.

"1397?," one says "circa 1394," one says "about 1400," and one says "1400?"

(3) As for the date of his death, three give it as "1468?," one (more confident) as "1468," and one as "circa 1467."

The most confusing thing about Gutenberg is that his name was not really Gutenberg. It was Gensfleisch. Again, however, there is disagreement, some saying it was Gänsefleisch. Whether Gensfleisch or Gänsefleisch, it seems to be his mother's family name rather than his father's. Moreover—and this is what I like most—it means "Gooseflesh."[1] Anyhow, the thrill of knowing all

[1]In my excitement about this I almost forgot to mention that in one book I found the spelling "Guttenberg." Of course this could be one of those typographical errors referred to above.

Johann

Gutenberg

The Happy Bookers

this should give goosepimples to any librarian, and perhaps ganderpimples to the Head Librarian.

Gutenberg was born in Mainz, Germany. He lived for a time in Strasbourg, borrowed money from Johann Fust to pursue his experiments with printing, was sued by Fust to get his money back, with interest,[1] went bankrupt, and all in all lived an exciting life. In addition Johann Gutenberg or Johannes Gensfleisch or Henne Gänsefleisch changed the lives of authors, publishers, booksellers, librarians, and readers by printing books by the letter instead of by the block. Books began to pour out of the printing presses, and there was more need than ever for librarians as well as support for libraries, some of which were not built to hold such a weight of volumes.

Gutenberg's masterpiece is the Gutenberg Bible. Many get the impression from this that Gutenberg wrote the Bible, but actually he only printed it.[2] It is also known as the 42-line Bible, which must have been a condensed version. Later they got it down to 36 lines, which is comparable to carving the Lord's Prayer not on the head

---

[1]Fust was not only interested but insistent. He was a printer himself, in fact at one time Gutenberg's partner, but it didn't occur to him to print currency instead of books.

[2]Again scholars differ. Some think Fust should get the credit, or at least should not have given credit to Gutenberg, who was unable to pay him all the gulden he had borrowed. As for who was the inventor of movable type, try saying "Fust was first," over and over, and you may convince yourself.

of a pin but on the point.

After Gutenberg came printers in France, Italy, Holland, and all over Europe. In Spain they even printed a papal (possibly a typo for "paper") bull, which would have wreaked havoc had it been let loose in a china shop or even in a library, with librarians, especially those in red dresses, standing on their desks and screaming for help.

Venice became a center of printing, especially noted for Nicolas Jenson, a designer of type faces,[1] and Aldus Manutius, who published small, inexpensive books. According to one of Manutius' biographers, he had the ingenious idea that "books should be made so as to be read." He also believed that "the best books should be put into the hands of the largest possible number of readers." Obviously Manutius, had he not been busy running the Aldine press, would have been a librarian.

The books published by Manutius were not paperbacks, since they were bound in parchment-covered boards. However they were pocket size[2] and could easily be carried around by anyone who could read

[1]If a Venetian noticed Jenson staring at him, he was probably aware that Jenson was looking for a new type face. At one time Jenson worked in Rome, being especially interested in roman types.

[2]How large the average pocket was in the late fifteenth century, I do not know. But there is nothing constant about the size of pockets. Note today, for instance, the variation between the size of vest pockets and coat pockets. In general, pocket books are made to fit pockets, while pockets are not made to fit books.

The Happy Bookers

Librarians and the Birth of Printing

Greek or Latin and enjoyed such a popular work as *Hypnerotomachia Poliphili.* If he did not wish to buy it, he could get it from the local library, though he might have to wait his turn, all copies being out.

But Manutius did more than publish inexpensive, portable books. In 1500, right on the dot, he invented italic type. Less known[1] is his regularizing punctuation, for

[1]By those (all too many) who have not read the author's *On Your Marks: A Package of Punctuation,* which is dedicated to Aldus Manutius.

Papal bull

The Happy Bookers

instance straightening out the use of the semicolon and the question mark. But for Manutius, "the father of modern punctuation," an even higher percentage of librarians and their patrons than at present would be wearing bifocals.

Finally it should be noted that up to about 1600, books were considered so precious that special care was taken of them. Foxtails were employed for dusting[1] and aromatic herbs were used for fumigating. These herbs may not have got rid of bookworms and other bothersome insects, but they made a library smell good. Librarians who lived near a slaughterhouse or an open sewer could hardly wait to get to work.

[1]But only after they had removed the fox.

Special care

VII

More about Librarians and Printing

Most of the early books were in Latin or Greek, which put another strain, in addition to eyestrain, on librarians whose native language was English. It is true that they were not yet confused by the difference between the cataloging system of the British Museum and that of the Library of Congress, not to mention the Dewey Decimal System. But many an English librarian whose knowledge of classical languages was a little rusty must have asked more than once, "Why don't they print a book in English?"

Finally someone did just that. About 1475 William Caxton printed the first book in English. However he did it not in England but on the Continent, in Bruges. He had translated from a French translation of a Latin work[1] something he called *Recuyell of the Hystoryes of Troye*. Apparently he was unable to find a publisher and therefore printed it himself. This is something many a beginning author, forced to seek out and pay a vanity press, would give his eyeteeth[2] to be able to do. Caxton, by the

[1]Sorry, but this is as complicated as I can make it.

[2]Or some even more precious anatomical portion.

way, used a cursive gothic type, which sounds rather vile and indeed was known as the *bâtarde* or bastard style.

Later Caxton returned to England and set up a press at the Sign of the Red Pale, a red pale or a pale red probably being pink, and there, in 1477, published the first dated book in England, *The Dictes or Sayengis of the Philosophers.*[1] The next year he published Chaucer's *Canterbury Tales,* which had a somewhat wider readership, and was on his way. In all, he published nearly one hundred books, and any librarian in the late fifteenth

[1] As "Sayengis" for "Sayings" indicates, good printers are not necessarily good spellers.

century who had never heard of Caxton would hardly be considered Qualified.

When Caxton died, in 1491, his business was continued by his foreman, Wynken de Worde.[1] Librarians will appreciate the modesty of Wynken, who referred to himself in his works not by his name but as a "school-

[1]He was probably related to the Wynken of the firm of Wynken, Blynken, and Nod.

Humility

The Happy Bookers

master-printer." In his reprint of Caxton's *Chronicles of England* he not only maintained his anonymity but begged God to have mercy on his soul. It was almost as though he were doing something wrong in making a book available to readers. Comparable humility is rarely found in such latter-day publishers as Knopf, Doubleday, or Simon and Schuster. Nor is such groveling recommended to librarians, few of whom have inflated egos or delusions of grandeur.

In the fifteenth century there were many advances in printing throughout Europe. An intriguing sidelight on the birth of books was that they were created by a union of matrices and patrices. Apparently a matrix and a patrix got together and soon there was, in the language of printers, reproduction. The book was born full size, however, and there was no such thing as a baby book or, happily, an adolescent. Otherwise librarians would have had a hard time maintaining quiet and order, with little help from a leaden matrix.[1]

It is no wonder that books printed before 1500 were known as incunabula, or literally "in the cradle." The great libraries of today, such as the British Museum, the Bibliothèque Nationale, and the Bodleian, possess many volumes of incunabula. However the usual city or

---

[1] According to one historian of printing, when a matrix wore out another could be made by melting down the patrix. The family life of the early book gives one the shudders.

Incunabula

The Happy Bookers

county library rarely has even a single incunabulum. If it does, the librarian had better not let anyone sign it out or even put it out on Closed Reserve.

A great help to the librarian was the title page, which was a surprisingly late development. Apparently it was assumed that anyone would know, after reading a few pages, what book it was. Another useful device was the frontispiece, an illustration in the front of the book[1] that gave some idea of the subject and tone. When books had both a title page and a frontispiece, librarians were not quite so often asked by patrons, "What's it about?"

An interesting development in connection with printing which may have been of some help to librarians was the printer's mark. This was something like a trademark, and made it easy to tell at a glance who was the printer of a book. The earliest known printer's mark, in 1457, was the double shield of the firm of Fust and Schoeffer. The two shields, with stars and angular devices on them, hung from a branch. This hanging motif may have signified the dependence of printers on librarians and readers, or it may have meant that Fust and Schoeffer were just hanging around, ready to take on another printing assignment.[2]

---

[1] As contrasted with the backispiece, or colophon.

[2] There is also a macabre interpretation, made by a librarian, that I shall not go into. "Hang those lousy printers!" she was heard to exclaim.

Many printers' marks took the form of armorial shields, knighthood still being in flower but starting to go to seed. Richard Pynson's three birds, easily recognized as chaffinches by anyone who knows what a chaffinch is, enabled librarians to impress their patrons by saying, "That is a book printed by Richard Pynson."

Mention might also be made of Gilles Couteau and his knives (or cutlery), P. Chandelier and, appropriately, his candle, Manutius' famous anchor and dolphin, and the curious, cryptic "W74C" of Caxton. There is some question regarding the significance of the 74, but I may be the first to point out that what is really important is the W.C., especially in time of dire need.

Though there was no best-seller list in the fifteenth century, the Bible was undoubtedly the favorite book. Since many people had their own copy, or knew someone who had one, it probably was not the book most signed out at libraries. But there was much demand for such religious tracts as the *Art of Righteous Living and Dying.*[1] Nevertheless, though they may have blushed a little and risked disapproving looks from the librarian, there were curious young people and dirty old men who took out the works of Chaucer and Boccaccio.

We have now reached the Renaissance, when horizons were widening. Also widening were librarians, some of them from overeating and others from the ruffles

[1]What intrigued readers was how to die righteously.

The Happy Bookers

and numerous layers of petticoats they wore. Among the great printers of the sixteenth century were Henri Estienne and Geofroy Tory, the latter known for introducing the apostrophe, accents, and the cedilla into printing. It is hard to believe that readers got along without the

Horizons were widening

cedilla for so many years. Imagine, whether or not you are a librarian, running into the word "facade" and pronouncing it "fakade," whereas merely by writing it "façade" it was obvious that the "c" was to be pronounced like an "s."[1]

Following these printers came Claude Garamond, Christophe Plantin, and many others. It was Plantin who proved that a publisher can also be a businessman. By combining printing, binding, and publishing he made a good living and is the envy of many a librarian even to this day. It was Plantin who published the eight-volume *Polyglot Bible,* which was not only full of glots but gave librarians a new cause for worrying about shelf space.

By the end of the sixteenth century, according to one historian, "books were pouring out of the presses in a flood." Librarians, always to be counted on and ready for any emergency, were there with their buckets, and then with towels and blotters when they got the books to the library. There was not a dry "I" in the house.

[1]It is ironical that Geofroy Tory hadn't a cedilla to his name.

VIII

Librarians after the Renaissance

Having survived the Dark Ages, the Middle Ages, and the Renaissance,[1] librarians now had a period of relative calm. They were busier than ever, though. With the development of printing there were more books to catalog and shelve, as well as more readers coming in for a book and making unpleasant remarks if the library did not possess it. Books being not only more available but easier to read than manuscripts, more people were finding it worth taking the time to learn to read. Throughout Europe, especially in France, literacy was becoming as widespread as gonorrhea and syphilis.[2]

Since there were more readers, there were also more authors writing books for them. The effect of this on librarians was that an Author Index as well as a Subject Index was inevitable. It was becoming increasingly diffi-

---

[1]The time not only of Shakespeare but of the "whole man," which must have been quite a shock to librarians who previously had seen only part of their male patrons.

[2]You might be interested to know that "syphilis" comes from (that is, the name of it comes from) a Latin poem by Fracastoro, *Syphilis sive Morbus Gallicus,* published in 1530, the hero of which is a shepherd named Syphilus.

Busier than ever

The Happy Bookers

cult for a librarian to remember the names of all the authors—something that once had been easy. Now there might even be two authors with the same name, including the same middle initial, and some method of identification was necessary. It is doubtful that fingerprinting was considered, since it was not used until the

Shrewd trade

nineteenth century.[1]

[1]Thumbprints were used by the Chinese long before the birth of Christ, but they were slow being adopted in the Western World. It remained for an American, Henry Wadsworth Longfellow, to suggest "Footprints in the sands of time." However this was rejected by librarians familiar with the shifting nature of sand and wishing something more dependable.

The Happy Bookers

National libraries began to flourish in the seventeenth and eighteenth centuries in Europe. If there were no national librarians, there were, as there are today, rational librarians. An example of a national library was the Bibliothèque Nationale in Paris, which started with the library of the royal family and expanded through purchase, gifts, and seizures.[1] French missionaries in various parts of the world preached against covetousness and as a result brought back many a coveted volume. Diplomats sent to foreign countries shrewdly traded a bottle of wine or a dozen feelthy postcards for a rare first edition. During the French Revolution, revolutionists seized the libraries of royalists who, having been beheaded by the guillotine, were not likely to do any more reading.

Thanks to such vigorous means of accession, the Bibliothèque Nationale became so large that the librarian found it necessary to divide the library into four main collections: theology, canon law, civil law, and belles lettres. The librarian in charge of the second collection was constantly having to turn away persons in military uniform who sought a book on the care and maintenance of artillery pieces.[2]

[1] A patriotic Frenchman on his deathbed, having a seizure, might be talked into giving his books to the Bibliothèque Nationale.

[2] This is not quite so ridiculous as you might think. After all, the word for "cannon" in French is *canon*.

Another national library is what is now the Salty-kov-Shchedrin State Library in Leningrad.[1] This was known as the Imperial Russian Library of St. Petersburg until the Revolution, and according to a Russian count it was at one time the largest library in the world. What is interesting about this is the count. The Saltykov-Shched-

[1]How to pronounce that "Shch" still has me baffled.

Catherine the Great

rin was begun with a Polish library, captured by Catherine the Great, that was run by two Counts, Andreas and Joseph Zaluski. Later Count Alexander ("Beef") Stroganoff was appointed director, and soon after him Count M. A. Korf was named librarian. Who came after Korf, I don't know, having lost count. Librarians will be quick to notice, however, that Count Korf had an M.A.

Even Switzerland started a national library. Oddly enough, it specialized in books on Switzerland.[1]

Along with national libraries, university libraries grew in number and size. In fact a university such as the University of Paris developed specialized libraries in such fields as arts and sciences, law, and medicine and pharmacy. This meant that librarians also had to specialize. A librarian who had been trained in philosophy, for example, was not very useful in a medical library, and might even become ill from reading about illnesses.

The invention of printing had made so many low-cost books available that some students owned their own books. This relieved librarians to some extent, though it complicated their lives in another way. They had to be more cautious about reprimanding a student for underlining and writing notes in the margin of the book, since it

---

[1]If this seems perfunctory, a more detailed treatment will be found in Marcel Godet's *La Bibliothèque Nationale Suisse, son histoire, ses collections, son nouvel édifice,* Berne, 1932. This exhaustive study runs to 46 pages.

might be the student's own copy. Caution also had to be exercised[1] when a student was seen departing from the library with a book that had not been signed out. It was still some centuries before anyone thought of posting signs reading: "Leave All Books and Papers Outside."

It is not known precisely when the word "holdings" came to be applied to the books in a library, but it may have been at English university libraries in the early seventeenth century. At first there was some confusion, since the holding might refer to two students holding hands, or even a student and the librarian.[2] But at university libraries in Scotland, such as Glasgow and St. Andrews, there was no doubt that holdings were the books the canny Scottish librarians held on to for dear life.[3]

As we have seen, national and university libraries developed early. However public libraries, in the modern sense of the word, did not appear until the nineteenth century. The first public library in the United States was founded in Peterborough, New Hampshire, in 1833. The fact that public libraries came so late may explain the

[1]The work of a librarian being sedentary, it was good to have even this much exercise.

[2]Highly unlikely during the period of Oliver Cromwell and the Puritans, but prospects brightened under Charles II.

[3]It terrified a Scottish librarian to think that the cost of lost books would be deducted from a salary which, hard as this is to believe, was even smaller than a librarian's salary today.

The Happy Bookers

continuing struggle of public librarians in America for prestige.

It was not until still later that the Delivery Desk, which suggested the obstetrical ward in a hospital, was changed to the Circulation Desk, aptly named because

Masquerading as a Cavalier

by running around and around it librarians could keep up their circulation. Some also refer to the Charge Desk, headed toward by librarians as they shouted "Charge!" and began their final sprint.

We have seen that there was censorship, the bane of librarians, as early as the ancient Romans. It reappeared in England under the Puritans, derisively called Roundheads by the Cavaliers because of their short haircuts.[1] The librarian knew at once, when a person with his hair cut short came into the library, that certain books should be put out of sight. These might, however, be the very books the Roundhead was after, though he would usually take out such books under an assumed name and while wearing a wig, complete with ringlets, masquerading as a Cavalier.

Despite all this, it was during the seventeenth century in England that a blow was struck against censorship by, believe it or not, a Puritan. True, this was a rather unusual Puritan, John Milton, a man who enjoyed fencing, riding, wrestling, and military maneuvers, was married three times, and stopped going to church. In his *Areopagitica*[2] Milton said such things as "as good almost

[1] Today such a person would be called not a Roundhead but a square.

[2] The full title, matching the length of its sentences, is *Areopagitica; A Speech of Mr. John Milton for the Liberty of Printing, to the Parliament of England.*

kill a man as kill a good book" (that "almost" causing one to breathe a little more easily) and "a good book is the precious life-blood of a master spirit, embalmed and treasured up on purpose to a life beyond life." Though this latter statement has been challenged by morticians, it has long been quoted approvingly by librarians.[1]

Let us now turn to Puritans of a somewhat different sort, not Roundheads but (some of them) Soreheads.

[1]See also Wordsworth's "Milton! thou should'st be living at this hour." Though Milton is not, his books are, and what he said about censorship has not been censored, for which librarians can be thankful.

Milton

IX

Librarians in Colonial America

It is not known whether there were any librarians on the *Mayflower*. If there were, they had little to do during the 65-day crossing but snatch a book away from a seasick Pilgrim before anything happened to it, or answer the request of a forgetful passenger who asked, "Have you seen my Bible? I'm sure it's on the ship somewhere."

Of course there had been an earlier settlement in Virginia, where a librarian would have found a wider variety of reading matter—fewer Bibles and a larger number of how-to books on how to hide from the Indians and what to do when scalped.[1] Once the Virginia colonists learned about tobacco, librarians had to be on the alert lest books be torn apart to furnish the wrappings for cigarettes.

The leader of the Virginia colony, Captain John Smith, is said to have had his life saved by Pocahontas, daughter of the Indian chief Powhatan, who interposed her head between Captain Smith's head and her father's deadly war club.[2] An equally implausible story is that a

[1] Call a surgeon and tell him to bring his scalpel.

[2] The "Pow" in Powhatan gives some idea of the way the chief could bring his club down on the head of a hapless victim. It was always a tense moment, unsettling for any settler.

librarian interceded, shielding the valiant Captain's head with a book. It was not, however, a copy of Captain Smith's as-yet-unwritten *The Generall Historie of Virginia.*

But back to Massachusetts. Many Puritans who left England because of religious intolerance became

How to

The Happy Bookers

intolerant themselves. Witches were burned, people were put into stocks,[1] and in at least one instance a young unmarried couple received a fine of twenty shillings for the crime of kissing. Librarians had to be careful about the books they possessed and recommended. *The Bay Psalm Book* was safe, as was the *New England Primer* as well as anything by Increase Mather, Michael Wiggles-

[1]Common stocks, for ordinary people. It was much later, with the founding of the stock market, that people went into stocks willingly.

Intolerance

The Happy Bookers

worth, or Jonathan Edwards.[1] A librarian who suggested a book by someone not a preacher was taking a chance and might wind up wearing a scarlet L.[2]

The first libraries were private libraries, the largest of them owned by ministers and doctors. If a library consisted of only one volume it was usually a Bible. If there were two books, the second might be something like *Directions for Planting Mulberry Trees,* which had been carefully censored for anything sexy, such as a reference to seeds. For a library of one or two volumes it was not considered necessary to employ a professional librarian, or at least not full time.

There were more openings for librarians with the founding of college libraries. The first was that of Harvard College, in 1638. It started with 380 books, given by John Harvard, and must not have had a very large library staff. The library grew, however, and by 1775 was large enough to require strict regulations. For instance the librarian was required to keep the library open and heated on Wednesdays, and only junior and senior students could take books out. However unusual latitude, as well as longitude, was shown in the rule permitting one

[1] *The Bay Psalm Book* was the first book printed in the colonies, in 1640. It must have been the word order in such a line as "The Lord to mee a shepheard is, want therefore shall not I" that made it so popular.

[2] This could indicate either "librarian" or "libertine" or both.

book at a time to be kept as long as six weeks.[1] William and Mary, whose last names I have forgotten, also had a library, founded in 1693. So did Yale, what later came to be known as Columbia, and Princeton. Any college without a library was almost as rare as a library without a college. Sometimes the librarian was known as the "keeper," but there was nothing nasty about a kept book.

No one was so important to librarians in colonial America as Benjamin Franklin. Remembered by others for flying a kite in a thunderstorm and for eating one loaf of bread and carrying two others under his arms as he walked down the street in Philadelphia,[2] he is remembered by librarians for quite different achievements. They know him as a printer, a publisher, a writer, and founder of the first subscription library. This last was in Philadelphia in 1731, financed by a group of readers who paid a membership fee and annual dues.[3] However some members could not have read the books in the library but for another achievement of Franklin's: he invented bifocals. More than that, if the library caught fire its readers could

[1] For such fascinating information I am indebted to Elmer D. Johnson's *A History of Librarians in the Western World,* now available in Japanese. How he learned such things I shall never know.

[2] Proof of both his hunger and his dexterity.

[3] That anyone would pay to read a library book is beyond the comprehension of the modern library patron, who thinks signing a card demanding enough.

be grateful to Franklin for having formed the first Philadelphia fire department and helped establish the first American fire-insurance company.

Well rounded

Among other things, Franklin invented a heating stove, did research in weather prediction, reorganized the postal system, was a colonel in the Philadelphia militia, served as a member of the Continental Congress, helped draft the Declaration of Independence and the Constitution, and was minister to France. Had he also been a librarian he could be considered a well-rounded man.

Now a brief pause for the Revolution, during which Minutemen were not, as might be supposed, speed readers.

X

Librarians after the American Revolution

After the Revolution, developments important to librarians came thick and fast, instead of thin and slow. For instance the Library of Congress was established in 1800 so that our nation's leaders could read the latest books and see whether they were mentioned in them. It also enabled them to pick up some good quotes they could use in speeches in the House and Senate.

An ingenious help to librarians in the Library of Congress was a book tunnel and endless-chain system that carried books to and from the Congress. There is no evidence that a librarian ever became entangled in the delivery system and wound up, faithfully clutching the book being delivered, on the floor of the House.

Books burn easily, whether they are burned on purpose or by accident, and librarians are therefore always worried about fires. Nor is a book much helped if a stream of water is played upon it by a fire hose. There are those, notably librarians and bibliophiles, who look back wistfully to the days when books were made of stone or baked clay. The only hope for the future would seem to be printing on waterproof asbestos.

The reason for the above reference to fires is that

the Library of Congress was burned by the British in 1814, and all the books were destroyed. One historian says the library was "burned under the administration of James Madison." This would suggest that either (1) Madison supervised the burning or (2) Madison and his cabinet were on the roof of the building at the time. Both

Picking up quotes

The Happy Bookers

possibilities are rather unpleasant and must have lost Madison support among librarians.[1]

But all librarians should be grateful to another

[1]If the second is correct, Madison undoubtedly lost the support of the library, and one wonders how he and the members of his administration escaped to run the country for three more years.

President, the great Millard Fillmore, who in 1851 helped save the Library of Congress in its second destructive fire. Fillmore, who did not own a book until he was nineteen,[1]

[1]The first book he purchased was a dictionary, no doubt to help him read books he borrowed from the library. In case you are interested, Fillmore's father owned two books, a Bible and a hymnal.

Bucket brigade

formed a bucket brigade with the members of his cabinet and managed to subdue the fire. The expressions "Pass the buck" and "The buck stops here" probably go back to this important event in American history, and should really be "Pass the bucket" and "The bucket stops here," immortal words uttered by President Fillmore at the head of the line.

Madison may have had a hand in framing the United States Constitution, but Fillmore should be held in greater affection by librarians. What good does it do to frame the Constitution if there is no wall in the Library of Congress to hang it on?

It should also be noted that the Library of Congress began the practice of printing and distributing catalog cards. Some ingenious librarian thought of turning the words around, and that gave us the card catalog. Librarians are constantly turning through the cards in a card catalog, which is why one of the requirements for a librarian is sturdy fingernails.

Public libraries in the United States received a boost, and so did the tax rate, when state laws permitted local governments to levy taxes to support public libraries. This began in 1849 in New Hampshire, and soon people in Massachusetts and other states were paying for public libraries whether they used them or not. The tax collector now became as much involved with books as the book collector, and the ordinary citizen became a collector's item.

The first big city library was the Boston City Library, which opened in 1854.[1] Many prominent Bostonians made gifts of books, and the Mayor himself made a cash donation.[2] The library grew so rapidly that it was necessary to engage an experienced librarian, Charles Coffin Jewett, who, according to Elmer D. Johnson, "had made a name for himself as librarian of the Smithsonian Library in Washington."[3]

Even with the involuntary help of taxpayers, there would not have been enough money to build all the libraries needed, and pay librarians, but for gifts from wealthy donors. Some, like John Jacob Astor, remembered libraries in their wills, and librarians went around humming the tune, "Thanks for the Memory." But it remained for one man, Andrew Carnegie, to give to libraries on a large scale (apparently weighing the money rather than counting it) and while he was still alive and might conceivably need to look out for himself in his old age. Moreover, and this is hard to believe, he was born in Scotland.

As a youth, Carnegie was very poor. At one time

[1] This was before the jacket blurb, "Banned in Boston," propelled many a book to the best-seller list.

[2] He may have had no books, or none he cared to have the public know he had been reading.

[3] There is a famous Coffin family in New England. Perhaps Jewett liked to remind the members of his staff, half-jokingly, "You are working under a Coffin." It made them squirm.

The Happy Bookers

he worked as a bobbin boy in a cotton factory, perhaps bobbin up and down in front of the loom. He earned $1.20 a week, which was even less than a librarian was paid. But he later went into other enterprises, such as working as a telegraph operator, and by the time he was twenty-four had made a fortune from investments in the Woodruff Sleeping Car Company.[1] Subsequently he went into the steel business, and one biographer says of him that "his steel plants grew rapidly." Librarians and others who have benefited from his wealth should be grateful that he discovered this means of producing steel, perhaps while experimenting with seedlings in his garden.

Carnegie began his philanthropy in 1901, when he donated $5,200,000 to the city of New York for the erection of 65 branch libraries.[2] During his lifetime he gave more than $43,000,000 to establish libraries, and this was only the beginning. I do not know the cause of his death, in 1919, but suspect he wore himself out trying, unsuccessfully, to give away all his money. How-

---

[1] "Let sleeping cars lie," said those who counseled Carnegie against taking such a risk. As any Reference Librarian could tell you, you have only to look up "Let" in the index of Bartlett's *Familiar Quotations* and you will learn that the original of this statement, referring to dogs instead of cars, can be found in Chapter 39 of *David Copperfield*.

[2] The idea of branch libraries obviously appealed to Carnegie after his success with steel plants. Since his wealth in 1901 was estimated at around a half billion dollars, he probably carried five million or so around in his pocket as small change.

ever the Carnegie Corporation picked up the ball, or the wallet, and is still trying. Carnegie libraries now number nearly 3000 in the English-speaking world, and some librarians are said to have amended their prayers slightly, saying "Carnegie be thy name."

By the latter part of the nineteenth century, if not earlier, women greatly outnumbered men as librarians. Indeed the librarian as a woman became a Stereotype, which has nothing to do with typography. However men continued to occupy certain positions, notably those that were (1) at the upper administrative level, whether or not actually on the level, (2) higher salaried, and (3) with shorter working hours. Increasingly, women objected to what they considered discrimination, but they were so well schooled (in Library School) that they raised their voices only outside the library, where readers would not be distracted.

With growing specialization, special libraries have developed in the past century which provide unusual opportunities for librarians who are qualified. A few examples of such libraries are the New York State Lunatic Asylum Library, the Sing Sing Prison Library, the International Ladies' Garment Workers' Union Library, and the National Livestock and Meat Board Library.[1]

There are also newspaper libraries, the most inter-

[1]Any applicant for a library position at Sing Sing must be able to carry a tune as well as a book. As for the Meat Board Library, it would be interesting to attend a board meating.

esting part of which is the morgue, which is not quite so gruesome as its name would suggest. Indeed it contains much more than information for future obituaries, and a librarian can work there alone, well into the night, without getting goosepimples.

Prison library

The Happy Bookers

Worse troubles

Even more important, associations of librarians began in 1876[1] with the founding of the American Library Association. It sets standards, issues publications, and, most important, holds conventions where librarians can temporarily forget their troubles by hearing of the worse troubles of others. The A.L.A., as it is known by librarians, was followed by such organizations as the Special Libraries Association and the Osteopathic Library Association.[2]

A few years later, in 1887, the first library school in the United States was organized at Columbia University. Eventually it became necessary for anyone going into library work to obtain a graduate degree in Library Science. What was really needed, of course, was a degree in Library Science Fiction, and this may come yet.

One of the courses in Library School is The History of the Book, in which it is hoped this book, which could not have been written had the author not read books written by authors who had read more books than the author of this book, will be required reading.

---

[1]This is not to say that librarians did not associate with one another previously.

[2]Whether there is also an Extra-Special Libraries Association I do not know, nor whether there is an Association of Library Associations.

XI

Librarians and the Dewey Decimal System

The idea for the Dewey Decimal System came to Dewey when, as a student at Amherst College, he was listening to what has been described as "a long sermon" by the college president.[1] It is not known what the president of Amherst said that gave Dewey the idea and led him to publish, in 1876, a 42-page booklet entitled *A Classification and Subject Index for Cataloging and Arranging the Books and Pamphlets of a Library.* However the length of the sermon may have suggested to Dewey the length of the title he first gave to what has since been shortened, by busy librarians, to "Dewey Decimal Classification," "Decimal Classification," "Dewey," "DDC," "DC," and "it."

Dewey published the 1876 version of his system anonymously. He may have been modest. Then again, he may have been uncertain about what he had done, or a little ashamed. Had he not attached his name to the 1885 edition, we might now refer not to the Dewey Decimal System but to the Anonymous Decimal System, or ADS.

[1] Is there any other kind? At any rate it gave Dewey time to think.

Deweys All

George

John

Tom

Melvil

The Happy Bookers

Nonlibrarians confuse the Dewey of the Dewey Decimal System with Admiral Dewey, who uttered the famous words, "You may fire when ready, Gridley" during the battle of Manila Bay; with John Dewey, the educator-philosopher-psychologist who developed the theory of "immediate empiricism," which I would explain if there were space;[1] and with Thomas Dewey, who twice ran for President and wound up on top of a wedding cake. One thing all four Deweys except Admiral Dewey had in common was some connection with Columbia University. What is probably most confusing, in any attempt to identify them, is that all four wore mustaches, Admiral Dewey's being the longest and Thomas Dewey's the shortest.

Melvil Dewey, who has been called "a many-sided genius," was born Melville Louis Kossuth Dewey but, always thoughtful of catalogers and knowing the smallness of catalog cards, shortened it to Melvil Dewey. Apparently it did not occur to him to go all the way and make it M. Dewy.[2] It is said that Dewey devoted himself

[1]And if I understood it.

[2]Anyone who heard him say "I am Dewey" must have thought it was I. M. Dewy.

Worked fast

The Happy Bookers

to simplified spelling, and not only of his name. It could be, however, that his spelling was the result of too much reading of the humor of Artemus Ward, Mr. Dooley, and Josh Billings.[1]

An example of Dewey's spelling, or dialect, is this, which he wrote in 1926 about his system. He refers to the earlier "confuzion that seriously cripld usefulness" and tells us that "work of previus librarians was larjly lost." "This sistem," he goes on to say, "wud enable each to stand on the sholders of his predecessors."[2] He closes with the remark that "All who contribute to the stedy improvement of future editions may know that they ar helping to make stil more useful a sistem. . . ." That shud make any gud librarian hapy.[3]

Before going into the Dewey Decimal System (and perhaps never coming out again), let me say something further about Dewey the man. Dewey lived to be eighty, though he writes in his diary of being "often in il helth, with tifoid fever, cof, and catar." On his seventy-fifth birthday he disclosed the secret of what he called his perennial youth: "It is becauz I have from childhood

[1]Cross-cataloged under Charles Farrar Browne, Finley Peter Dunne, and Henry Wheeler Shaw.

[2]A delicate balancing act and hard on the librarian at the bottom, probably the most recently hired.

[3]Uzers of Dewey's sistem jeneraly ar of another skul of thot about speling.

always workt fast and long hours, but hav never worrid. I hav always been a total abstainer from liquor, tobacco, tea, coffee, and condiments, and hav been a small eater and a larj sleeper."[1]

What he means by being a "larj sleeper" is not that he increased in size during the night but that he usually slept for exactly ten hours. He was so fond of the Decimal System that, as he put it, "I even like to sleep decimally." Those who heard him say this thought he said he liked to sleep dismally, and tapped their heads and smiled knowingly. Had they understood what he really said they would still have tapped their heads but would have been unable to force a smile.[2]

The basic difference between a librarian and a non-librarian is that a librarian understands the Dewey Decimal System. And yet it is very simple. It requires only a knowledge of all recorded knowledge and the ability to divide by ten. The system, you see, is divided into ten classes which are in turn divided into a hundred divisions which are then divided into a thousand

---

[1]Despite his reference to being a "small eater," it is said that while he was at Amherst, working on his Decimal System, he "devoured all possible literature on libraries." Apparently it was high on information but low on calories.

[2]For most of this biographical material I am indebted to Grosvenor Dawe's *Melvil Dewey*, 1932. Anyone who claims to have read this scholarly work in its entirety is not to be trusted.

The Happy Bookers

sections. There is really nothing to it, which explains why, in the seventeenth edition, the explanatory matter is limited to the Publisher's Foreword, the Editor's Introduction, and the original Introduction by Melvil Dewey—

Very simple

in all taking up only 108 pages. One is then ready to plunge into the System itself, the fundamentals of which run to merely 1146 pages more.

For some reason, however, only a librarian can tell you at a glance that 721.044 73 refers to a book on architecture involving the use of copper and that 551.515 3 will get you a book on the dynamics of the mechanics of meteorology. The easiest part of all is 000, which is Generalities. It is only when you get to 001, having to do with Knowledge, that things begin to get a little more complicated.[1]

Though the Dewey Decimal System is the oldest and most widely used, some prefer the Bibliographic Classification of Bliss, the Colon Classification of Ranganathan, or the Expansive Classification of Cutter. There is also the Top Secret Classification, for books kept under lock and key.[2]

Much else might be said about classification systems, but out of deference to Melvil Dewey we ar going to keep this gyd simpl and eazy.

---

[1] It is possible that 000 is really "0! 0! 0!" and is the exclamation of a librarian who has found a book missing, though a book that is found that had been missing would elicit the same response.

[2] Books not under but on Locks and Keys can be found at 683.32.

XII

Librarians Today and in the Future

Librarians have come a long way since stone and baked clay tablets, hieroglyphics, Ashurbanipal, rolls of papyrus, parchment codices, Pisistratus, Tyrannion, the *scriptorium,* Gutenberg (or Gänsefleisch), Caxton, Manutius, incunabula, Benjamin Franklin, Andrew Carnegie, the founding of the A.L.A., and everything else treated so thoroughly[1] in the previous chapters. As Melvil Dewey would put it, "Hyly important chanjes hav been numerus."

Of recent years, the image of the librarian as a little old lady in tennis shoes has changed drastically. She has come a long way. Now she wears shoes with high heels that enable her to reach the topmost shelf. Or, if she is really "with it," she may wear sandals.[2] More men are librarians and some are in subordinate positions, though not insubordinate. It is not enough to be merely a librarian, but one must be a reference librarian, a cataloger, a children's librarian, or an audio-visual specialist. Also a

---

[1] If not exhaustively, then exhaustingly.

[2] Secretly she may imagine herself in an ancient Roman library, hoping the Emperor will drop in and she can get his autograph.

She's come a long way.

The Happy Bookers

librarian can be in a university library, a law library, a public library, a medical library, an armed services library, a prison library, and on and on or, for the part-time librarian, on and off.

As with paramedical personnel, there are more and more paralibrarians, not to be confused with a pair of librarians. The paralibrarian has no library degree and, just as her medical counterpart is not permitted to perform surgery, should be careful about doing any reader's advisory or reference work. Presumably giving wrong advice might lead to a malpractice suit.

The work of librarians has necessarily changed because of changes in libraries. College and university libraries, for example, now have carrels. These are unlike Christmas carrels in that they are used the year around.[1] There are also rooms for showing films and slides as well as soundproof recording booths and darkrooms for developing photographs. Some of these rooms have dual-purpose uses, a room for showing films also being useful for lectures and for putting on plays and puppet shows for children. However the darkroom is not recommended as a place for reading.

[1]The word "carrel" for a small enclosure or alcove is also spelled "carol" by architects, and "carol" comes from the Middle English word for dancing accompanied by singing. In fact it goes back to the Latin *choraules,* a flute player who accompanied the choral dance. Librarians would, I am sure, discourage singing, dancing, and flute playing in the modern carrel.

Extended services of some school and public libraries necessitate that librarians handle many items in addition to books: motion picture films, filmstrips, slides, transparencies, overlays, disc and tape recordings, projectors, record players, tape recorders, cassettes, viewers for individual use, multimedia kits, etc. Whereas formerly nothing could upset a librarian more than loss of a book, now there could be such disasters as breakdown of a film projector, finding a crack in a record, or discovering a gap or erasure in a tape.

All of this means that a librarian is no longer fully prepared by Library School courses such as "Bibliography and Reference Sources," "Basic Cataloging and Classification," and "Administration of Libraries." Now the librarian must also take work in "How to Splice a Broken Film," "The Operation and Care of Tape Recorders," and "The Underlying Benefits of Overlays." Some librarians, proud of their open-mindedness, who were never shocked by a book, are shocked by a short circuit in the electronic equipment.

Many librarians have been unionized. They may have joined the union of a library staff, or government employees, or of plumbers, carpenters, or electricians. They had long used the union catalog, but now they carry a union card as well.[1]

---

[1] They joined a union either by choice or by being outvoted. "In the union there is strength," they were told by union officials.

The Happy Bookers

Disastrous breakdowns

Indeed the change has been so great of recent years that some libraries are no longer called libraries but are known as Learning Resource Centers or Media Centers. Librarians, however, are still generally known as librarians and not yet as Learning Resourcists or Media Centerists, though this may be only a matter of time.

A twentieth-century development has been the bookmobile, which permits librarians to take books to those who are unable to get to the library. The bookmobile also makes it possible to get outdoors and go for a spin into rural areas, especially enjoyable in the spring and fall. Though I have been searching the police rec-

ords, I have been unable to find the driver of a bookmobile booked (an appropriate term) for speeding or drunken driving. There must be something about that precious cargo that keeps librarians on the straight and narrow and, when necessary, on the curved and narrow.

So much for librarians of today, though no refer-

Proper glasses

ence has been made, among other things, to the interlibrary loan, the *Library Journal,* or the *Horn Book.*[1] Let
us now turn briefly to libraries and librarians of the future.
This, it must be confessed, is purely speculative, since
even the most thoroughly researched reference books
give no clear picture of what conditions will be like in
another fifty or one hundred years.[2] Even the foreseeable
future is hard to foresee.

The way things are going, however, it would seem
that microfilms will become micro-micro-microfilms, and
a page can be reduced to the size of the head of a pin.
According to John David Marshall,[3] an important service
of the librarian will be to direct the library patron, before
he peers at the micro-micro-microfilm screen, to the
resident optometrist (or ophthalmologist) to secure the
proper glasses. On leaving, the reader will be provided
with a seeing-eye dog to help him home.

But what will the librarian of the future be like? In
order to cope with the minuscule microfilm books that
have been forecast, the librarian also may have to be

[1]This last will be a disappointment to anyone wishing information about the trumpet or the tuba.

[2]One book in this field that seems accurate and soundly based
is John David Marshall's *A Fable of Tomorrow's Library,* Peacock
Press, 1965. This scholarly work runs to seven pages, including the
title page and copyright page.

[3]*Op. cit.*

The Happy Bookers

reduced to a comparable size, at least during working hours. This might be accomplished by scientific means or, more literarily, by using the technique Alice learned from the caterpillar in *Alice in Wonderland*. Thus the librarian before starting work would eat a piece of mushroom held in the right hand to become smaller, and at quitting time would eat a piece held in the left hand to become larger. Just who on the library staff or the Library Board would be identified with the White Rabbit, the March Hare, the

Dial a book

The Happy Bookers

Mad Hatter, and others will perhaps vary with the library.

This is assuming, however, that there will still be flesh-and-blood librarians amidst the microfilmed books in the computerized library or Center for Storage and Retrieval. It is possible that librarians will be robots, controlled by Master Minds having mastery of a master computer at the Library of Congress.[1]

Or there will be no libraries and no librarians, flesh-and-blood or otherwise. The onetime library patron will press a button and turn a dial on his TV, whereupon the requested book, in the desired language, will appear on the screen, the pages turning at the designated speed. The only interruptions will be commercials in which authors plug their latest books. These they will have produced with electronic typewriters that, when set to WRITE, will produce overnight a novel, biography, juvenile, or whatever the author has programmed.

Then again, as some old-fashioned members of the literary community hope, authors will write much as they do now, books will be books, libraries will be libraries, and librarians will be librarians.

Then science, helping but not taking over, can concentrate on finding a cure for the common cold, which sometimes keeps librarians away for a day or two from the work they love.

[1]These Master Minds may, of course, also be robots, operated by a superior race on a distant planet.

About the Author

Richard Armour has led a double life. As a scholar he has a Ph.D. from Harvard, has held research fellowships in England and France, has lectured or been guest-in-residence on more than 300 campuses, has written "publish-or-perish" books of literary criticism and biography, and has lectured for the State Department throughout Europe and Asia.

As a popular writer he has written more than 50 books of humor and satire, in prose and verse, and has contributed over 6,000 pieces to the leading magazines of the U.S. and England. His syndicated weekly feature, "Armour's Armoury," appears in more than 300 newspapers. He is perhaps best known for his fact-based spoofs of history and literature, hailed as "classics of American humor."

He is married (to the girl he met in first grade) and lives in Claremont, California.

About the Illustrator

Campbell Grant was with Walt Disney for twelve years as a character creator and story man, and has done the drawings for the book version of many Disney films, as well as having illustrated a host of other books for children and adults. Since 1960 actively interested in archaeology, he has made extensive studies of the rock paintings of American Indians and has recorded and made paintings of the originals. His studies have resulted thus far in five published books, including *Rock Art of the American Indian,* the definitive work on the subject. He and his writer wife live on, and tend lovingly, an avocado ranch near Santa Barbara.